FLOWERS THAT DIE

FLOWERS THAT DIE

GIDEON HALPIN

Poems

atmosphere press

Contents

dedicated to the beings
under relentless attack of demons
who find rest in written word

Mid-daydream

sad boy wistfully strolls mid-daydream
through a wild poppy meadow

butterflies alight on soft brown curls
"fly me away" says he

they flutter him in paths
of breeze

(rainbow kisses sky)

sits on a branch
honeycomb in hand
he munches bread and cheese

(see the branch bend and toes ripple grass)

thinks of a girl
who
like the rainbow is gone
leaving clouds alone in the sky

with no place to be
sad boy drifts as a leaf
in a stream

Night Goes On

brick walls and wooden beams
hold a worn wooden bar
lit by candles
casting shadows as mirrors
while the faithful gather
huddled over tables
rattling together as dice in a cup
and the night goes on

going to bed
birds exit the day
leaving rats to scuttle below
and the fishy breath of the docks
salts the breeze
murmurs of the city echo
trash cans, car alarms, and voices oozing in and out of windows
where TVs glow as lighthouses
and the night goes on

constellations of street lights
shine as a map
viewed from a hillside chateau
and like a dagger
the smell of doughnuts and pastries
rips the somnolence of dark
the night goes on

stars navigate the ocean of heaven
slowly fading out to a deep blue horizon
a mood ring for the sunrise
and the night is gone

Song of the Lost Heart

make me into a mountain range
unflinching with buttresses of sheared basalt
sloped with sighing pine maidens

the heart I gave you frolics as a colt
it is not of lifeless stone
do something with it!

if I were the moon
how beautiful my solitude would be
and my scars, a revered imagination

the sky is not your kingdom, but the ground
I set you among the many
find your beauty in the people

how majestic are the summer lakes!
the wildlife lap the ripples and butterflies romp to and fro
why can't I be as the lakes?

the lakes I've formed and measured
but you have not those boundaries
for that you should be thankful

Greenhouse

sun in the sky
shadows of birds
on the ground fly by

air holds its breath
with inhale and exhale
sail the sailboats and kites

tremors the earth
while the runner runs
tremors the earth
as it runs under the runner

fire in the fireplace
shines bright
fire in the fireplace
is the sun in night

bark surrounds edges of trees
bark falls off
just like leaves

bees build homes
in the holes they bore
bees hide their young
from the outside world

life is a garden
in a greenhouse of glass
time seems forever
until it has passed

Sad Boy and the Moon

falling as a dying breeze
rippling as last rays of evening
akin to a pebble
tossed in a pond

sad boy stumbles home

dead weeds among gravel
dust whisks by

sad boy is alone
empty bottle in hand

good morning good evening
blackbirds are gone
oak tree has fallen
rubber swing sobs in the grass

in a dry creekbed
toads groan among ruined poplars
young vultures try their wings

sad boy slumbers in the wayside

night asks wind
"play a song in the hollows"
wind caresses leaf and branches
a satin lullaby

sad boy sleeps as a tombstone

across the stars walks Orion
patrolling for trespassers
on the moon

moon bends down
to nudge the sad boy
beetles scatter in the light

leaning on a dream
boy stands tall
stretching arms as sails

wind rushes through the hollows
a rattling wave of desolate
boy sidesteps tornado
kisses the moon on tip-toe

Orion departs
shaking dust off his sandals
boy gleams as comets
sling through the sky

Eyes of a Grandmother

For Chloe

light blue window frames
light pink door
in the headlock of a dull white wall
look across a turquoise sea

oxidized, the colors
laugh in joy
the eyes of a grandmother
telling children stories

tales of deep, dark woods
stories of bears and blackberries
of knights, towers, and blonde hair
or beautiful young days
with her lover
who snores opposite
still clutching his cane

sometimes in a whisper
it seems as sand
has fallen from an hourglass
into her voice
and unable to explain
the tears in her eyes
I look out the window
to play

Tall Drink of Water

pheromones fill the room
like a fart in a photo booth
cute as you are I need air
and as much as I want space
I want a pair of hands
to run through my hair
and lips to kiss down my body

a tall drink of water
you are
I am
as sweat drips down my sides
can I carry a waterfall like you
in my breast pocket
or cartwheel in your heart?

Thumb War

I am flipped over the shoulder
like a sack of potatoes
carried by whims I don't own
and worry some time it'll rain
if it'll rain it'll flood
and knock apricot scent from the air
it's like a thumb war
with an older brother
if you win
you'll get bopped on the head
it's the way it is
when I forget how to fly
dreams from the ground
forgotten they drown
or get bopped on the head
or taken to bed
by fake laughs and fake hair
crucified by fake nails
and nothing's quite there
just a bump on my head
or a sore thumb
and I wonder
why ain't I flying?

Farewell

Lady of the mountains
smiling silhouette
my shadowy daydream

you've slipped past

if I missed you
sorry

to pick a boquette
I was in the valley
and to bring you a vial from a star
I shivered in the night sky

because you leave no trace
at each river crossing I wait
commanding the cairns to keep watch
to tell the tidings of my heart

attaching a megaphone to each echo
I call
without reply waiting

alas, I shall leave this mountain
and frolic in the valley
between fields of daffodils
and dark iris hedgerows
where the meadow stream sighs
and stars call upon me to play tag

Dream of the Boy

alders grow
boundless of grove
down where the river goes

boy sits on a rock
counts clouds like a clock
chewing a stem of grass

the girl all alone
has run from home
skipping to him as a stone

they meet on the edge
of society's hedge
and build themselves home

To the Woman with Beautiful Eyes

her eyes
cut through
as light in dark

my shadows
afraid
leap across the room

hand trembles at my thigh
like the pitter-patter of a code sender

I forget words to say

I'm moved as chimes in wind

her touch is music
to my skin

dreams shimmer
as rivulets from my eyes

her fragrance
as soft rain in eucalyptus
when the land is dry

River

rocks ripple silken river
pines hold green
while oak leaves burn

in the river, Father
I saw a woman in the water
smooth and sleek
as the stones beneath her feet

wading ankle then knee-high
she glowed softly as starlight
bathing in sun and water

cheeks blushing as the sunset
I tug on my heart
as a leash
lest it be gone forever

Porch Lamp

I pretend
the porch lamp
a moon
and my tummy's gurgle
a heart flutter
I wish you to replace my shadow

the crickets
and crawling dirt monsters
sing ballads
to each other
rubbing wings
and such

if I could
but
slap my side
and
flick my thighs

use body odor
as a megaphone

I'd be
the smelliest leaping creature
on your doorstep

Blankly Stare

dry was the wind
twirling your hair
tossing it past turned shoulder
and whipping against
cheeks and eyes
as if strands of water
ran down your windows
dark hair flowing
was watching underwater waves
make intense love
to a kelp forest

sometimes
I forget you speak
and blankly stare
as if you were the ocean

Oranges

I'd like to bring you
a box of sunshine
but a crate of oranges will do
if they make you smile
if whenever you eat an orange
you think of me
then I wish
the sun itself was citrus
that I could peel and section
just to share with you

Skeleton

oh I could have been a leaf!
sunny green with my lovelies
bathing naked in morning dew
but the maze I love is made of jasmine
she is a secret to discover
beneath charcoal balconies
turquoise eyes bright and slashing
tear down my facade

I want her in the orchard
night flung open like wind blown linen
at my touch a river
I hold the moon in my fingers
I feel the moon within her bosom
and each kiss is molten metal
poured in my skeleton

Striped Blanket

stripes run the blanket
like bars in a jail or zoo
and as animals in a hollow
we nestle like foxes

static in dry wind
your skin on my skin
legs as vines entwined

what is the flavor of your lips
that I must keep tasting?

hearts in rhythm beat
each breath is one
and your hands on my body
drizzle as honey
while a full moon peeks through the window

Silhouettes

clothed in starlight
dancing
in the rooftop garden
cheek to cheek
each breath is one

streets below shimmer
broken bottles
and bubblegum
guide the way home

they move and twirl
stepping close
as two shoes tied together
cadence of night
whispering voices of wind

Converse are scuffed

unable to afford cologne
he wears a smile

soft as satin sheets
flowing in the air
fresh from the local thrift
her dress moves as an eel

ambient sirens moan as an echo
trapped in a jar
seeming less than a generator's hum

maybe to the movies
maybe just a stroll down the street
it might be coincidence
when eyes meet
his heart skips

something familiar about her beauty
reminiscent of a childhood toy
is an adrenaline shot of exuberance
not felt in a decade or more

falling into each other like an armchair
gauging a smile with a stare
words of love whispered is a wager
paid for down the line

dancing together
starlit in beauty
two silhouettes on a city skyline

Exhale of a Flame

I threw a stone of worries
ocean rippled
sky put its roots
in my lungs
whispering silent cries
ice plants breathe ocean dawn

I painted a flower on your window
like the exhale of a flame
iron stove toasts sage
rubber boots and corduroy
inside from the rain

Pacific rocks and frothy waves
clouds in moody heart locket
I'll keep you close as a worn $20
snuggled in jean pocket lint

Gas Chamber

pocket blade
stretches its leg
plunges through bread
and chaperones
Brie to the elopement

picnic blanket
picked from the backpack
which now folds inward
like a deflated balloon
or a vacated colon

the grass beneath
crying when crumpled
shouts aromas

if we were in a gas chamber
I'd tell you I love you
instead of watching
fluffy clouds
floating the sky river

the problem is
without you
I feel like a podless pea
and when we leave this place
I'll feel like that again

Dolphins

dolphins swim in my soul
the ocean
pumps life's elixir
tides of wonder
enchantment
utmost content
buoy the spirit
from the mysterious deep
as if to swim
amidst the star-filled heavens

the warmth of night
and sternness of moon
draw me to the vast
unknowable expanse
and in that ancient dark
the spirit of God
still moves
upon the face of my waters

Casa Shambala

flowers drink inside glass bottle
candles in sand in jars
smokey music caresses
incense drenched air

my love will find her way
through dark rain
my love is an ocean
is a marble full of color
my love my love I call her

words like matches
start the flames
curtains sway softly
back and forth again
from the shadows on my walls
it seems the moon
has filled my room
the perfect greys and whites

Harmonica

let's build a driftwood fort
and cast our dreams
for over the horizon
a silk boat waits
like a jailhouse harmonica
you're familiar to my mouth
beautiful in sonnet and verse
tongue weaves ear-licking words

drunk from you and the rum
unable to repress the urge
I see the world in your eyes

Prayer Flags

prayer flags hang on the laundry line
everyone's prayers hanging out to dry
makes me fine can't tell you why
to see sheets blow in the wind

I had true love but didn't show up
spent most of my life getting stuck
carried the darkness never giving up
the things that were hustling me

What's going on would never be
if Marvin kept testing shade trees
he made a mirror so we could see
what's really happening

sometimes I think I'm the only one
torn between shadow and seeing the sun
hollow feelings in the man I've become
the dandelion blowing away

I talk to God like drinking green tea
it's a bittersweet form of energy
to play your cards knowing the
king of heart must bow

Serpent Heart

my notebook is a urinal
pen pisses in my journal
I drop in black ink
heavy sinking thoughts

feet finally
start to walk calmly
but in the darkness of
my serpent heart
eyes watch me

pressing against
the bars and gates
leading to escape
eyes of fear
eyes of love
I hate them all because
something seeing me
adds torment to misery

Walk

ripped jeans and barbwire dreams
ants bite ankles of dusty feet
road drifts out of sight
behind a rise to the right
my dry clay mouth
cannot contour the words you need
I squint in afternoon sun
and swallow tears

I wish I could go
to the tower of flowers
and stand in the fragrant shade
breeze under arms and sky over head
bright birds flying like dreams in my bed
simple earthy house and simple wooden walls
filled deep in color
deep enough for stars
steaming bath in cool dusk
sweet olive oil skin
standing in my doorway
your frame
I want to embrace you
unflinching as a park bench
holding your many forms
I want you to overflow the bathtub with me
and listen to a storm

in healing waters I hold my breath
above the surface I rest
my bottled words float the ocean
with nowhere to go
I best be going
keep walking walking walk

Lost Coast

on a grey, cloudy day
evening falling
sky to black
I tune to static

(ocean swims in ears)

easing down the driveway
oversize tires command obeisance
to rows of bowing grass

the cabin stands in front
unromanticized by lively colors
or youthful renovation
and as the bitterly beautiful coastline
it remains
haggard, worn, and moss covered
like a bounce house starting to deflate
backs of rafters stoop
resembling an overloaded clothesline

new blood returns
in the place of the ancient
wearing my father's coat
I am no stranger
and the woodpile, well covered
has waited
and sings to me a welcome
within its cracks and pops
and in warmth
old walls shift like bones
adjusting in a continuance of sleep

from a distance
the flickering firelight must seem
a twinkling eye
amid squinting wrinkles

By Will or by Wind

a sparrow wipes its beak
on the railing
as if cleaning a blade
and its colors match
the weathered porch varnish

silently
plants are eaten by insects
yet their hope buds forth
to follow the light above
splitting concrete
and growing roots through walls
leaves falling in season
fading as a perfect dream
by will or by wind
they won't be seen again

and the woodpeckers bore holes
the eaves their voodoo dolls
storing sack lunches for winter
or perhaps to aid a traveler
weakened
the roof caves

in the shade of an afternoon
children play in the grove
swinging on dead grapevines
once strangling the branches of trees

they fall and fly with innocence

Words

if words could weave a safety net
or grow soft green grass
I'd say them all
some sweet thing to caress a dream
kindness to catch a fall
or perhaps playful and romantic language
the kind that bites your ear
for I love the way your eyes shimmer
you, whose laughter sounds like rushing water
yes, it could be
there are words unsaid
but time will uncover
the well from which they spring

Roses of Our Love

love will rekindle
though Cupid's bow is broken
and all his arrows shattered
against our hearts of stone

your eyes have no horizons
nor ships of salvation sailing
nor disease of Columbus
to end this sickening affair
they remain
as a green and vibrant garden
where the roses of our love
once again may bloom
amidst the thorns we wove
around each other's necks

Bird

girl floats in the garden
see her dress
ripple in breeze
stands as a windmill
chin to the sky
wishing herself a bird

sees the boy walking in denim
smells the stink
of underarm
he plucks a stunning flower
and tosses it away

girl wishes herself a bird

KDS

in the North
there's a girl
soft as moss
on the sitkas where she roams
picking mushrooms
wildberries
and searching rock walls as an eagle

rooted in the wilderness
she claims the sunshine
swims with otters
and drinks clouds from the sky

armies of sighing hearts
trample meadows
and with binoculars search
asking pines and cedars
and studying ferns for a trace

empty they return
for she is a mole
traversing the ground of her choosing

Pebble

dark was the candle
swirled by draft
the light not reaching the rafters
seemed a balloon hit by a toddler
and the shadows barely shadows
hid amongst the black surround

on the table
incense ashtray lighter
candlestick for a moth campfire
on the ground
stars look down
through the skylight as a keyhole
and I write a letter
building with words
a perfect pebble
to throw at your window

Baby Blue Skies

when wheat fields lose
their wheat to the snow
and sleeping on the floor
worry rises to snuggle your dreams
you will see a bald raven
old from the years of heralding doom

without a creak or shudder
you must leap
strap on wings
and carry a torch in your teeth

memories will guide you
of two souls lost in a room
restless as water
dropping the length of a downspout
and clanging inside your head

look for me in a house of mirrors
where I cannot see my heart
but beyond eyes
I sail on fluff with you
amid baby blue skies

Soul Drumming

dark and mysterious drumming
endless, haunting melody
without form
eludes
without form
overpowers
exotic crimson feel
bloodred sacred sunset
way of the wind
shifting wings
volumes yet to be written
the melodies songbirds sing
canyons and valleys
nightly night stark naked
voids of the soul
awaiting exploration
trees made for shade
suffer saw and blade
yet in buckets collect
their tears of pitch
and turning into boats, sail
or become homes and temples
after crucifixion with nails
the sharps and flats
climbing high to fall back
whether marching or dancing
footfalls are music
in the unknown drumming of soul

Canyon

I want to talk to the wind
and no one else
in the canyon with deep reply
where banks are sharply carved
and I hear my footsteps echo
before dawn
when the sun begins to peek
under the dark threshold
like a light in the hall
while the world tries to sleep
and the smell of grass
and the smell of dew on grass
witness

expressions of affection
are no longer floral
for I've left the bouquet of flowers
attached to their branches and roots
a rose would do you no good
why would I bring beauty
to where it abounds
when I know just what you want?
a caress constant as constellations
and a kiss colored in sunset
and a dream unscorned
will I give you
and if you do not believe me
my friend the wind
will carry echoes without end
until you hear every word

Petals

fling rose petals to season air
fling them upwind to embrace your hair
crimson flecks
in wavy black
a supple scent
to surround your smile

a walk in the woods
a mossy path
a hood of mist floats in the trees
heart twitches
and I feel as a bright green leaf
for the clasp of your hand
is light from a lantern
you I will not lose to the dark
and your eyes
like planets glow
brighter than any star

Paradise Valley

cloud glow
candle moon
shines upon the night
air is soft dough
sweeter than a cinnamon roll

shadowy ridges slump their shoulders
and shrug with waving trees
countryside is worn
water rounded rocks
and sloped knolls
seem a cemetery of mountains and streams

silence in the song
cicadas sing
announces your soft arrival
and the breeze brings perfume

as only a few stars
may peek through fog
nipples shine through your blouse
and cascading hair
is soft rain
tickling face and neck

while night itself
tucks beneath a blanket
your body covers mine as silk
and sleep as the sunrise
seems a distant voice

Night Ride

beats the hooves
on the skin of the earth
invites them in does the mud
cuneiform writing on the river's edge
and the night fills with steam
snouts of steeds
inhale and exhale dreams
two abreast they ride
past marshy reeds and apple trees

sweaty thighed on smooth leather
feeling every twitching tendon
and leaned over the necks
as if to nuzzle the mane

Sketch of a Cabin

hands in her lap
Sasha sits by the fire

last year's forest
heats the kettle

singing in anguish
water dies
its ghost forming a cloud

winter shivers
knocks on the door
peers through windows
scuttles through the chimney
rustles the flames

saw hangs over doorway
a guardian
a guillotine
its form echoes
in planks and walls

freckled with rust
it rests

cabin as a cradle
rocks in the wind

puffing itself
as a hedgehog
bread tans its delicate skin
soon to be hewn
as the planks

smell leaks through the chinking
taunting the hunger of winter

Fog

maracas dangling from the roadhouse wall jolt a tune
each time the door slams
and it slams each time
its coiled spring
withdrawing it to the frame
as a child
publicly embarrassed
runs and clings to the leg of a father
or cries behind the dumpsters
miserly trapping the heat
it closes itself off

two shuffle inside
shoulder to shoulder
eyes cutting to the narrowest detail
knowing the world is suspect
and life to be mistrusted
as a bitter igloo
built on splitting ice

in a far corner
hunched as a cloaked monk
stooping over dusty volumes
a bearded, smelly creature fingers the local paper
as one might sort foreign coins
or count a debtor's balance

eventually it grunted
calling out the latest foreclosure
directed to the man behind the delaminating counter
who did not incline to hear

the two walked from the bar
their usual liquor in hand
moving to the window
to keep watch

more trickle in
by ones, twos, and threes
no one turns
at the clap of the maracas

haggard, stooped, and rapidly aged
the sinuous and the dirtily corpulent
pass as fairgoers through a turnstile
out and back and in and out
through the beating heart of the roadhouse
languid and fragile
as dominoes
waiting their time to fall
before the conspiring world
shrouded in fog

Needle

arrows of man
fletching of feathers
the blade and bone
seen through the all seeing
eye of the needle
where in a maelstrom
of rattling volleys
one may, perhaps
with a string
thread itself through
and weave
the broken, threadbare
and ripped seams
the wore-torn violence
of a sad life
where melancholy
with hammer and anvil
strike
flattening dreams
dissolute and cankered

where lovely memories
are but laughing spectors
the morning prayers dim
and robins cease to sing

larceny of time
emptying the vault of the soul
where the heart can be heard
ripping itself in pieces
like screams in the night
and mothers shield the eyes
of their children
should one fail to mend the moment
should one fail to thread a needle

Big Sur

somewhere above this vaulted ceiling of fog
the sun tries to peek
as a child prying the finger gaps
of his mom's hands
the lusty earth
forbidden from sight
and I
standing as a mountain off Highway 1
gaze hawklike at the waves
throwing their bodies against the rocks
while the coastline stands as Tiananmen tanks

the wind tugs at my coat and pants
salty air
sweet to the breath
and the sound of exhales are lost to applauding waves
and rattling gravel

to my back stand sequoias
centuries more to revel the view
and in prudent silence
sway in the gusts

hand around the waist
I pull her slightly closer
a woman who visits my daydreams
and on tip-toe kisses my cheek
eyes stop gazing
and my fingers tingle like lightning rods
I feel the weathered asphalt
through the soles of my shoes
and the voice of my friend
as he calls through a cracked car window
like a hermit crab in a surging tide

bones quiver as resonating cymbals
and suddenly we dive back
to the wind shelter of the camper
and a quick look over the shoulder
watches it all fade to memory

Voice

fits to the form
like pockets in jeans
she holds precious things
and lips answer
from the heart's bedchamber

in evenings of spring
sometimes I've seen
her talking to blades of grass

smile is a firefly
and I love to watch
her hips as she walks
so simple so sweet
a honeysuckle scent
a longing of youth

sometimes alone
I create a mountain
but when the lost sheep is found
it sinks to the ground
and I go to the sound of her voice

Waves

smooth curves
slick
with jagged edge
glimmer in deep green
like snapped wine bottles
in a mirrored hallway
row upon row
they lunge and tumble
until crawling prostrate
on the sand
though fingers claw
their bodies are dragged
into the gaping mouth
swallowed
and spit back
those smooth curves
slick with jagged edge
glimmer in deep green

Terrace View

glowing with fading strength
the sun lies down beneath the waves
like a tired hamster
it nestles
a light minty green floats
atop striated sandstone skies
and a gecko scuttles along a rafter
for a last bath in light

on the uneven concrete floor
sand and dust play tag
hiding from breeze in cracks and pocks
and to the girl
lying with chin on folded hands
ocean ripples seem as a flat grass mat

suddenly
a sliver of moon appears
like a lover
late for a tryst
it follows the lantern of the sun

Ships

ships line the shelves
of an ocean view room
and the feather duster
caresses them softly
for it knows
the feathers of which
would rather be flying
and the rose boutonnière
lying on the dresser
desiccated and still
would go to the ground
to sprout once more

among these I stand
if I could sail
or take to the wing
I'd be reborn to you

Dream Sweet

hammocks sway and summer breeze
gently folds the valley
trees wave their hands
as if goodbye
softly though the sun has gone

sky loses color
and doves are mournful flutes
the day has fled
yet the stone bench
holds the heat like a locket
closely as a dream
afraid it will be forgotten

the night is coming
falling as dust on a fresh swept floor
worn and scuffed
the country slowly turns
a dance led by the stars
they twirl
dew drapes the air in satin
a cloak upon the garden
and flowers close their windows

Donkey's Dream

in the donkey's dream
earth is a boundless garden
turning under the sun

wind swats flies
and streams run
as their young

grass combs hair
and dew alights on eyelids
a soft caress at dawn
gently, birds wipe their feet
and massage
talon and beak
perched on the spine as a mountain

beauty of flowers fills the eye
beauty of flowers fills the belly
beauty of flowers renews each day
as if night were a magician
and in pathways filled with rocks
hooves play hopscotch
stepping in open space

Saint Judas

in the floodplain of the city
discreet as the scent of burning hair
Saint Judas and his bag of tricks
dwells on the edge of the vineyards
between the scrub oak hills and trash ravine

gathering the drifters
pulling them as a poultice on an open wound
he seems
like the son of God

smooth and lithe as a willow branch
slippery as an eel
his jaws are brass pliers
and planets burn in his eyes

ardent as a wild boar
he seemed to me
a certain man named Death
bucked clean from his apocalyptic horse
with the demeanor of a self-impressed child

he takes pride in his footfalls
is wiser than a serpent
and seven times more charming than an enchanter

snatching fate from the abstract
he clenches it in his palm
or perhaps stowes it in his bag
a moldy thing
smelling of kerosene and rotten fish

maybe there are tarot cards inside
silver coins or oaths of the dying
definitely hallucinogens
the bag bulges as a leperous tumor
either dangling over his shoulder
or slumped at his feet

if you care to see him
bring your own means of salvation
and a dagger on your thigh
for now
he dwells on the floodplain near the vineyards

Dust

dust hitchhikes on dusty feet
finding its way inside
a house a sock a shoe
exploring an old vacuum
years gazing into a starry sky
yearning to feel the pull of space
finally, it has arrived
travel by water
travel by wind or broom
search the rootworks of a plant
and the juicy, luscious fruit

perhaps a weekend in a cobweb
or an eon in a Persian rug
leaving imprints of footfalls
a map of what became
immersing itself in pottery
or ovens made of clay
yes, the humble on the ground
rule the earth without a crown

Dark Skin

you need dark skin
under the sun
and if you're white
it's a sin
to stoop so low
to break your back
for the strawberries and the vineyards
and a few laborers
were drenched in sweat
pants and long sleeves on
working from the age of six years old
to provide for family
and the day was hot
but a moment of shade
Champagne bottles popped
from a hot-air balloon overhead
but their work did not stop

The Nations, The Wildflowers

the flag flows proudly
behind a lazy RV
as if to conquer the desert
but it hasn't gone far
it sits in the plain
surrounded by parked cars
near the toilets
the nations the nations
are gone from before
if the desert was barren
it was cauterized before
layers to the slumped hills
like layers on a wind-whipped banner
proclaim the country's true colors
ridgelines lay bare
as rocky worm castings
perches for the wind
and the wandering soul
whom time will erase
and dust will recover
for the red rocks burn
through the cobalt speckled sky
where clouds have not dulled
nor belittled the land
in its authoritarian shade of gray
under which the flagpole stem
offering its wildflower
to eminently fade
as so many have before
the nations the wildflowers
they appear in their seasons
while unyielding red rock
burns against cobalt skies

Storm

on a walk the lightning struck
landing its legs it struts
rain tackles dust
pinning it to the puddles
in mud it meets
its sisters and brothers

arched doorways and mud-brick walls sweat
perspiration slithers to the ground
pooling it mimics
sky and street

while thunder punches air
in cobbled alleys
dim and dark
laundry flees
a hobo to anywhere
its wings the wind
rips through chimes
and slams open windows

cats slink under eaves
and crawl inside crates and boxes
against the restaurant sides
whose blackboards begin to cry
words and figures flowing
rivers of beige mascara

unflinching, the pigeons
tuck their heads to their chests
and eyes peep through feathers as keyholes

Grove

amidst the grove
cedars   redwoods   pines   elms
her voice bends notes
song in slalom
weaving to my ears

immediately, a lawyer
my erudite shoulder dweller
briefcase in hand
adjusts reading glasses
and clears his throat
and with numerated lines
tells me bliss
is a ramification of her smile

yet my feet, earless
already skip
and I cannot hear knowledge
for eardrums joyfully play her song
and bodily
I am willed to her

Hourglass

sad boy is flipped back and forth
like sand in a glass

to himself never free

coaxing his soul to speak
he ties his tongue
(hear only crickets sing)

without mastery
his spirit runs from him
as a wild horse on the plain

(mane flows as a wheatfield)

far away dust rises
sun burns ochre behind

shackled to a chain
boy grinds his days as powder

week after week
he must work his forty hours

Dream of the Man

in the graveyard of architects
fall abandoned tree forts
collapsing as dreams
rubbed from the eyes of morning
yet westward remains
a stained glass window
tilted in rotting frame

droves of thrushes flit from wild sage
and humidity
the sun's magnifying glass
seeks to steam clean my clothes

fading to gold
the former generation
dedicates its seeds to heaven

and we stroll through the meadow
fingers combing the grass
like a trailing hand in water
or a farewell caress

suddenly she turns
glowing as an ember
sweeter than a chamomile breeze
linen dress and silken hair
waving against a still sky
while valley oaks
fill with songbirds

Home

rain cuts through clothes
soaked as the ground
I trudge against wind's prodding
to the broken mill and waterwheel
whose ancient timbers remain together
locked in chink as a rugby scrum

at the end of a slick stone path
I light a lantern and repocket the matchbook
creaking open the door
to slip past the threshold

eyes adjust

on the measure
a sharp saw portions pieces of lumber
to be sistered to rafters
or made into shelves
shining new against the framework
as grandchildren

a trusted carpenter's square passed from my fathers
aligns the work in my hands
the cadence of markings is music to me
each piece composed with a pencil

this will be our home
in the wooded district
a place where soft ferns grow
yet home of the heart
is the heart of my woman
and in my hearth she lights a fire

Twine

delicate copper lights
illuminate lawn
kept in form by blade

perimetrically growing
vibrant pink roses
taunt the conformity of grass

the dull electric glow
robbing darkness
an evening among the flowers

tied to a fence
they stand tall
while budding and blooming fulminations
lean from rigid posts and planks
trusting twine to withhold the fall

in spirit and in beauty
may you be as roses
in wonder reaching
floating and rippling

weightless in the air

and I shall be the twine
to keep you from the dust
the jealousy of darkness
as I hold you day and night

Dusk Falls

across the room
dusk falls through an open window
and lays in the floor
lush lips of rose
fading to dark shades of blue
the heat falls too
tea warms hands
but I do not sip
body sits as a army
waiting for a trumpet

while whispers of breeze
turn to shouts
small drops fall on the rooftop
as if a child threw pebbles into the air
silence
then steady drumming
thousands of hands
strike the tin drum skin

discontent in darkness
night flicks a faulty lightswitch
twisted veins of halogen flash
then, curtains of black separate
for an intermission to view the stars
yet before ground can breathe
with repumped squirt guns
clouds shoot down from a tall treehouse
then run
and thunder trundles on with empty caissons

before blending in with trees
the dancers catch a last gust
and take an exit bow

Rain

pensive clouds lift not their knitted brows
and obsidian skies
wring their garments dry
so children may splash in puddles

and the garden as a story
embellishes itself
adding verdant details
while birds gossip
the earth entire their tabloid

slick and damp
the bridge
will soon be a moss carpet
for little feet to cross
and throw twigs into the stream

I didn't mind before
because I love a column of sun
but it seems someone
has poked a hole in my roof

Dawn to Dusk

1*
like the tide in a sea cave
her body moves with each breath
golden hair covering the pillow like sand
sunlight coats the air
and hummingbirds float through the bougainvillea
while breeze sways curtain shadows

roses and fertilizer seep through humidity
like a sauna of fabric softener
rustling my hair with curls

2*
in the tiled grotto
ivy overtakes the ornate designs
now seeming a kaleidoscope

lining the winding walkways
clouded in dew like foggy car windows
lanterns hang
watching paths as prison guards

the compost pile holds secrets
plant spirits
waiting to be reborn
turning the old and young
until they are gone
one by one

3*
in the night
she comes to me bright
draped in the gilded moon
hair shimmering as spider strands
I brush them away from her face

planets in her eyes
she touches me gently
I hold her in grass and moss
while crickets sing
like static on a phonograph

Man

man couldn't choose his markings
not even the name he's called
watches men rise and men fall
feels the earth turn
and heart pump under his skin
the pressure of his tribe
and the icy wind
wants to live better than he has before
catches a glimpse into heaven
but can't get past the door
sees love, the beginning and end
watches stars cross and uncross
in the lives of his friends

sees beauty but it's cold to the touch
can't rely on love
can't control lust
never trusted his feeble intuition
said he was free
but lived like in a prison
thought the walls he was called to build
would fortify his mind
and keep him from getting killed
had to get strong
or he was fit to die
barely could run
but tried to fly

try to walk in his shoes
but the shoes won't fit
smell hits your nose
and you're through with it
let hair run long
man let his thoughts run deep

got clean cut but still can't find sleep
wants to return to the earth
or to the Lord
but he can't ask for mercy
when he lives by the sword

man hates to walk in the dark
but the lantern's broken
with only lightning for spark
gets tired of feeling alone in the world
gets tired of fighting in a circle
gets tired of the whirlpool in the water
laments his life and wants to die
but death comes when he's ready to thrive

doesn't want to sell his soul
but maybe just a part
enough to get ahead in the race
to satisfy his ego and still save face
enough to control the remaining soul
enough to know when to brake
to read the dice before they roll

man doesn't truly see the path
is given direction
but often just laughs
doesn't see the destruction to come
isn't fit to raise himself
let alone a son
blames the world for what he's come to be
studies himself in the mirror
but feels a mystery
thinks summer days are long under the sun
thinks he can wash his hands
when the day of death comes

Before Dawn

in the still before dawn
stars empty the sky's stadium
black fades to blue
and celestial chromatography
suggests the curfew of sleep
yet I sit at a rough wooden table
waiting for water to boil
and the horizon to steep in color

like a child in a theater
excited with anticipation
I strain for the sound of birds

coffee is a ceremony
conducted with reverence
a bishop at mass
amplifying the quiet

measuredly
I gaze about the cabin
the one in the cradle
will call me father
and my lover will later
call me by name
yet the only sound
is soft breathing

Memory of Longing (circa 2015)

mountains were dipped in snow
and paint-peeled gears
trundled me on an industrial porch glider
passing above laden evergreens
whose arms as fluffy canteens
held their next drink of water

I sat still on the lift
though my thoughts in circles wandered
as a hunter intent on his previous tracks
or wind blowing a restless merry-go-round
in orbit they were tethered
to the form of Eva
a nymph of beauty
her heart an open field

while all else was snow around me
I was warmed by my smitten heart

Sun Fall

when the sun falls
birds stop singing and fly
lightning bugs light their lanterns
and hide their dark disguise

atop the eaves
or in the tops of trees
a pair of young eyes watch
while calls in the garden
echo as crickets
searching for a lost child

the child slips down
the child is found
a tight hug warms the night

Slough

in the reeds past the hedge
lies a path
bent and muddy
whose oozing muck
swallows
dead and fallen trees
yet to the left
a canoe is stashed
with paddles inside

it is here, my son
we will go
bring the lantern with extra oil
and polish the panes
for the night
dark and silky
does not withhold mystery
hidden by day

we'll paddle the canoe
in the light of the lantern
we'll paddle the canoe by moon
passing statues of trees
with steaming air
sticking as cooked rice
wishing to be licked by breeze

look!
in the dark waterline
the eyes of frogs
when they shine
seem as kissing stars

the bats swoop by
watch their wings
row through sky
and with good ears
weed out insects
who sing out of key

and when you see the heron
asleep on its feet
watch
for it is not asleep
when proud eyes slip by
the bill will strike as a needle

but just before you tire
is the time I'll turn around
so you'll ask
if we can go again

Dream Ship

the boat under the oak
is a treehouse for children
held aloft on its trailer
no longer weeping
for the hole in its belly
because it will not sink
parked in the side yard
and for the young
dressed in tattered clothes
it is a ship of dreams
where the four year old
is not a child
but a fearsome pirate
a warrior with toy pistol
world at his feet
and sisters, wise
teach keen imagination

Vermont

plaster walls as lumpy snowfields
reflect morning glow
while rough cut pillars
like legs of a chicken
hold the beams
the wings
we nestle underneath
and inhale steaming tea
our bending lips float words
as soft clouds before sunrise
and your eyes are clear waters

Americana Summer

a looking glass ripples as jello
articulated by wind
the bow of a violin

still water

holds aloft parajumpers
fallen from a sky of cottonwoods
who line the banks as rice throwers
expecting the bride and groom

lounge chairs for turtles
the dead trees lay strewn

mud shoals carry travelers' tracings
from early in the year
mud shoals wait for rain
to make their scars disappear

on the opposite bend
under the willow
next to the elm
a Jon boat hides in the leaves
as if to jump out in surprise
but has now fallen asleep

cutting leaves of green
two boys clear brush
and hang a rope swing
with a knot at the end for their feet

tumbling
they leap
into the embrace of the stream

Bougainvillea

last year
I bent the hands of earth
and cupped them around the base
of a bougainvillea
to hold a stein of water
not merely a sip
and now it grows outside the door
with blushing leaf vanguards
protecting the flowers
as a naked princess
and each new burst of color
is the pencil mark of a child
drawn on a wall
to measure how tall they are
yet, when old and shriveled
fall

so I hold your heart
like roots of a vine
swimming in love and tears
and the kind words you say
bloom day by day
replacing the old
before they fade

You or Me

who with hammer, saw, and nails
makes a dead tree into stairs
or in a haunted forest
builds a house of light
can grow a garden of forgiveness
where lost souls find life

clothed in kindness
wears a smile
and heats the hearth
to sit and talk a while

whose shoulders you can stand on
whose shoulder you can cry on
who is a cherry blossom
pulling springtime on a leash
and sets ginger to boil
until the kettle runs over
filling mugs of friends
baptized in liquor

who will sail the streets of sorrow
awash in a flood of tears
sees the desolation
and with words tames fear

they could live among us
or descend from above
but it could be you or me
when we learn to love

Crumpled Napkin

until my face is a crumpled napkin
I will dance in the sun
with a breeze between my legs

until I blow away like a napkin
you can press me to your lips
until I blow away like a napkin

I want to glow and spin like a carousel
will you ride me up and down?
I like the way you feed me carrots
fresh from the ground
and the bright colors
you paint weathered benches

the way you mold to my body
is soft dirt to the bare foot
the way a finch loves a sunflower
you attract me like no other
like soft green grass
that will not cut me

I like a pool with no edges
I like to swim under the moon
it's like the rumble of a train
on a warm night with water cool

you are an oxygen tank
I explore the depths I fear
because I breathe easy
floating atmosphere

all good plans are made in treehouses
you're the hoot of an owl
not a car horn
for you
I'll let down the ladder

we are real flowers
that die

About Atmosphere Press

Atmosphere Press is an independent, full-service publisher for excellent books in all genres and for all audiences. Learn more about what we do at atmospherepress.com.

We encourage you to check out some of Atmosphere's latest releases, which are available at Amazon.com and via order from your local bookstore:

As a Patient Thinks about the Desert, poetry by Rick Anthony Furtak

Winter Solstice, poetry by Diana Howard

Songs of Snow and Silence, poetry by Jen Emery

INHABITANT, poetry by Charles Crittenden

Godless Grace, poetry by Michael Terence O'Brien

March of the Mindless, poetry by Thomas Walrod

In the Village That is Not Burning Down, poetry by Travis Nathan Brown

Mud Ajar, poetry by Hiram Larew

To Let Myself Go, poetry by Kimberly Olivera Lainez

I Am Not Young And I Will Die With This Car In My Garage, poetry by Blank Rong

Saints of Sacred Madness, poetry by Joyce Kessel

Thirst of Pisces, poetry by Kate March

Damaged, poetry by Crystal Wells

I Would Tell You a Secret, poetry by Hayden Dansky

Aegis of Waves, poetry by Elder Gideon

About the Author

Gideon Halpin didn't like to write until he was 18. Although he grew up hearing his father read poetry in the evenings, started devouring the King James Bible as a five-year-old, and took a keen interest in rap during high school, he didn't have the creative juice. His half-assed attempts at prose paled in comparison to the vivid street imagery of Tupac and he didn't find the wherewithal to use the word "bosom" as did the classic poets like Longfellow. What started the writing process wasn't inspiration but desperation. Faced with depression and stagnation, he started taking a notebook on his outings and found relief in beautiful thought turned to ink.

Halpin is a bartender, traveler, athlete, and adventurer. He is a veteran of spiritual warfare and internal conflict who seeks a simple life filled with joy and passion. His writing displays unadorned emotion with the beautiful and disparate woven together. *Flowers That Die* is his first book of poems.

Made in the USA
Columbia, SC
28 December 2021

52357589R00059